DISNEY'S THE HUNCHBACK OF NOTRE DAME

ILLUSTRATED SONGBOOK

Music by Alan Menken

Lyrics by Stephen Schwartz

ISBN 0-7935-6640-1

Wonderland Music Company, Inc. and Walt Disney Music Company

DISTRIBUTED BY

HAL•LEONARD® CORPORATION

7777 W. BLUEMOUND RD. P.O. BOX 13819 MILWAUKEE, WI 53213

CONTENTS

THE BELLS OF NOTRE DAME

THE BELLS OF NOTRE DAME

Music by **Alan Menken**
Lyrics by **Stephen Schwartz**
Latin lyrics adapted by **Stephen Schwartz**

Roughly, with force

Morn - ing in Par - is, the cit - y a-
Dark was the night when our tale was be-

wakes to the bells of No - tre
gun on the docks near No - tre

Dame. The fish - er - man
Dame. Four fright - ened

fish - es, the bak - er - man bakes to the
gyp - sies slid si - lent - ly un - der the

F/C   **C7**   **F**   **F7**

bells   of   No - tre   Dame.   To   the
docks   near   No - tre   Dame.   But   a

Gm   **Am**   **Dm**

big   bells   as   loud   as   the   thun - der,   to   the
trap   had   been   laid   for   the   gyp - sies,   and   they

Gm   **C/E**   **A**

lit - tle   bells   soft   as   a   psalm.   And
gazed   up   in   fear   and a - larm   at   a

Dm   **C7/E**   **F**   **B♭m/D♭**

some   say   the   soul   of   the   cit - y's   the   toll   of   the
fig - ure   whose   clutch - es   were   i - ron   as   much   as   the

bells,
bells,
the the

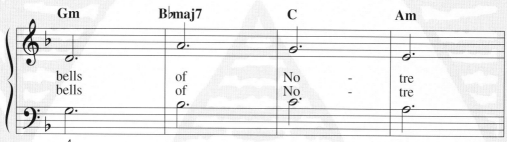

bells bells of of No No tre tre

1. Dame.

2. Dame.

THE BELLS OF NOTRE DAME

Music by **Alan Menken** • Lyrics by **Stephen Schwartz** • Latin lyrics adapted by **Stephen Schwartz**

CLOPIN:
Morning in Paris, the city awakes
To the bells of Notre Dame
The fisherman fishes, the bakerman bakes
To the bells of Notre Dame
To the big bells as loud as the thunder
To the little bells soft as a psalm
And some say the soul of the city's
The toll of the bells
The bells of Notre Dame

Dark was the night when our tale was begun
On the docks near Notre Dame
Four frightened gypsies slid silently under
The docks near Notre Dame
But a trap had been laid for the gypsies
And they gazed up in fear and alarm
At a figure whose clutches
Were iron as much as the bells
The bells of Notre Dame

CHORUS
Kyrie Eleison   (God have mercy)

CLOPIN
Judge Claude Frollo longed to purge the world
Of vice and sin

CHORUS
Kyrie Eleison   (God have mercy)

CLOPIN
And he saw corruption ev'rywhere
Except within

CHORUS
Dies irae, dies illa   (Day of wrath, that day)
Solvet saeclum in favilla   (Shall consume the
                               world in ashes)
Teste David cum sibylla   (As prophesied by
                               David and the sybil)
Quantus tremor est futurus (What trembling is to be)
Quando Judex est venturus (When the Judge is come)

ARCHDEACON
See there the innocent blood you have spilt
On the steps of Notre Dame
Now you would add this child's blood
   to your guilt
On the steps of Notre Dame
You can lie to yourself and your minions
You can claim that you haven't a qualm
But you never can run from
Nor hide what you've done from the eyes
The very eyes of Notre Dame

CHORUS
Kyrie Eleison   (God have mercy)

CLOPIN
And for one time in his life
Of power and control

CHORUS
Kyrie Eleison   (God have mercy)

CLOPIN
Frollo felt a twinge of fear
For his immortal soul

FROLLO
Just so he's kept locked away
Where no one else can see
Even this foul creature may
Yet prove one day to be
Of use to me

CLOPIN
Now here is a riddle to guess if you can
Sing the bells of Notre Dame
Who is the monster and who is the man?

CLOPIN AND CHORUS
Sing the bells, bells, bells, bells
Bells, bells, bells, bells
Bells of Notre Dame

OUT THERE

OUT THERE

Music by **Alan Menken**
Lyrics by **Stephen Schwartz**

Easily, in one

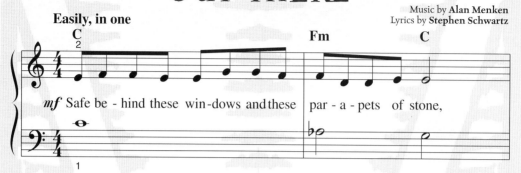

mf Safe be - hind these win-dows and these par - a - pets of stone,

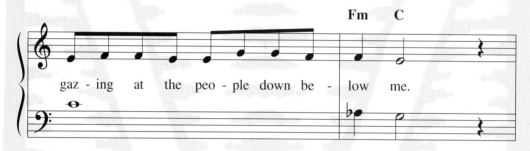

gaz - ing at the peo - ple down be - low me.

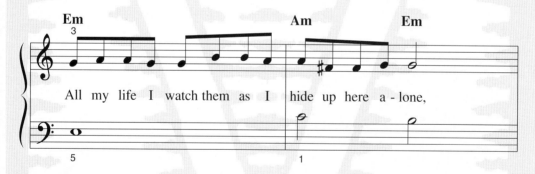

All my life I watch them as I hide up here a - lone,

hun - gry for the his - to - ries they show me.

All my life I mem-o-rize their fac-es, know-ing them as they will nev-er know me. All my life I won-der how it feels to pass a day not a-bove them but part of them and out there liv-ing in the sun.

F **F/G** **C** **F** **Eb**

Give me one day out there. All I ask is one to

Ab **Bb C** **F** **Em7**

hold for - ev - er. Out there where they all live un - a-

Am **Dm7** **Dm7/G** **Em7**

ware, what I'd give,——— what I'd dare

Am **Dm7** **F/E** **F6** **F/G** **C**

just to live one day out there.

OUT THERE

Music by **Alan Menken** • Lyrics by **Stephen Schwartz**

FROLLO:
The world is cruel
The world is wicked
It's I alone whom you can trust in this whole city
I am your only friend
I who keep you, teach you, feed you, dress you
I who look upon you without fear
How can I protect you, boy, unless you
Always stay in here
Away in here?

FROLLO:	QUASIMODO:
You are deformed	I am deformed
And you are ugly	And I am ugly
And these are crimes	
For which the world	
Shows little pity	
You do not comprehend	You are my one defender
Out there they'll revile you	
As a monster	I am a monster...
Out there they will hate	
And scorn and jeer	Only a monster...
Why invite their calumny	
And consternation?	
Stay in here	
Be faithful to me	I'm faithful
Grateful to me	I'm grateful
Do as I say	
Obey	
And stay	I'll stay
In here	In here

QUASIMODO:
Safe behind these windows and the parapets of stone
Gazing at the people down below me
All my life I watch them as I hide up here alone
Hungry for the histories they show me
All my life I memorize their faces
Knowing them as they will never know me

All my life I wonder how it feels to pass a day
Not above them
But part of them

And out there
Living in the sun
Give me one day out there
All I ask is one
To hold forever
Out there
Where they all live unaware
What I'd give
What I'd dare
Just to live one day out there

Out there among the millers and the weavers
and their wives
Through the roofs and gables I can see them
Ev'ry day they shout and scold and go about
their lives
Heedless of the gift it is to be them
If I was in their skin
I'd treasure ev'ry instant

Out there
Strolling by the Seine
Taste a morning
Out there
Like ordinary men
Who freely walk about there
Just one day and then
I swear
I'll be content
With my share
Won't resent
Won't despair
Old and bent
I won't care
I'll have spent
One day
Out there

TOPSY TURVY

TOPSY TURVY

Music by **Alan Menken**
Lyrics by **Stephen Schwartz**

Brightly

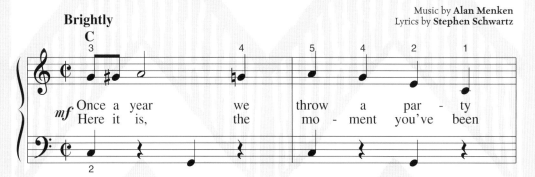

Once a year we throw a par-ty
Here it is, the mo-ment you've been

here in town.
wait-ing for.

Once a year we
Here it is, you

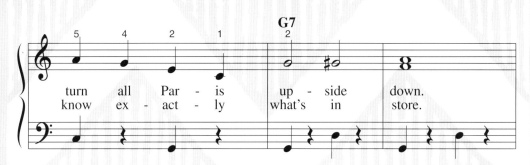

turn all Par-is up-side down.
know ex-act-ly what's in store.

Ev-'ry man's a king and ev-'ry
Now's the time we laugh un-til our

king's a clown.
sides get sore. Once a - gain it's
Now's the time we

C6

Top - sy Tur - vy Day. So
crown the King of Fools!

F

It's the day the dev - il in us
make a face that's hor - ri - ble and

Fm

gets re - leased. It's the day we
fright - en - ing. Make a face as

C/E

E♭dim

mock the pig and shock the priest.
grue - some as a gar - goyle's wing.

G7

Ev - 'ry - thing is top - sy tur - vy at the
For the face that's ug - li - est will be the

C   **E7**

Feast of Fools!
King of Fools!

A6

f Top - sy tur - vy! Ev - 'ry - thing is
Top - sy tur - vy! Ug - ly folk, for -

up - sy dai - sy! Top - sy tur - vy!
get your shy - ness... Top - sy tur - vy!

C#m

Ev - 'ry - one is act - ing cra - zy. Dross is
You could soon be called Your High - ness! Put your

F#m7

B7sus

gold and weeds are a bou - quet.
foul - est fea - tures on dis - play,

B7

A/E

That's the way on Top - sy Tur - vy Day.
be the king of Top - sy Tur - vy Day!

E7

A

21

TOPSY TURVY

Music by **Alan Menken** • Lyrics by **Stephen Schwartz**

CROWD:
Come one, come all!
Leave your looms and milking stools
Coop the hens and pen the mules
Come one, come all!
Close the churches and the schools
It's the day for breaking rules
Come and join the Feast of...

CLOPIN:
Fools!

Once a year we throw a party here in town
Once a year we turn all Paris upside down
Ev'ry man's a king and ev'ry king's a clown
Once again it's Topsy Turvy Day
Good is bad and best is worst and west is east
On the day we think the most of those with least
Ev'rything is topsy turvy at the Feast of Fools!

CROWD:
Topsy turvy!

CLOPIN:
Ev'rything is upsy daisy!

CROWD:
Topsy turvy!

CLOPIN:
Ev'ryone is acting crazy
Dross is gold and weeds are a bouquet
That's the way on Topsy Turvy Day

ALL:
Topsy turvy!

CLOPIN AND CROWD:
Beat the drum and blow the trumpets

ALL:
Topsy turvy!

CLOPIN AND CROWD:
Join the bums and thieves and strumpets
Streaming in from Chartres to Calais...

CLOPIN:
Scurvy knaves are extra scurvy
On the sixth of 'Januervy'

CLOPIN AND CROWD:
All because it's Topsy Turvy Day!

CLOPIN:
Come one, come all!
Hurry, hurry here's your chance
See the myst'ry and romance

Come one, come all!
See the finest girl in France
Make an entrance to entrance
Dance la Esmeralda...
Dance!

Here it is, the moment you've been waiting for
Here it is, you know exactly what's in store
Now's the time we laugh until our sides get sore
Now's the time we crown the King of Fools!
So make a face that's horrible and frightening
Make a face as gruesome as a gargoyle's wing
For the face that's ugliest will be the King of Fools!
Why?

CROWD:
Topsy turvy!

CLOPIN:
Ugly folk forget your shyness...

CROWD:
Topsy turvy!

CLOPIN:
You could soon be called Your Highness!

CROWD:
Put your foulest features on display
Be the king of Topsy Turvy Day!

CLOPIN:
Ev'rybody!

CROWD:	CLOPIN:
Once a year we throw a party here in town	Hail to the king!
Once a year we turn all Paris upside down	Oh, what a king!
Once a year the ugliest will wear a crown	Girls, give a kiss
Once a year on Topsy Turvy Day	We've never had a king like this

CLOPIN AND CROWD:
And it's the day we do the things that we deplore
On the other three hundred and sixty-four
Once a year we love to drop in
Where the cheer is never stoppin'
For the chance to pop some popinjay
And pick a king who'll put the 'top' in
Topsy Turvy Day!

CLOPIN:
Mad and crazy, upsy-daisy, Topsy Turvy Day!

 # GOD HELP THE OUTCASTS

GOD HELP THE OUTCASTS

Music by **Alan Menken**
Lyrics by **Stephen Schwartz**

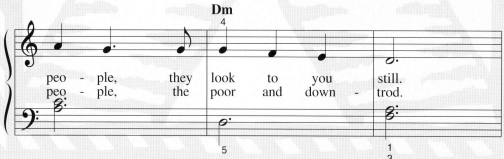

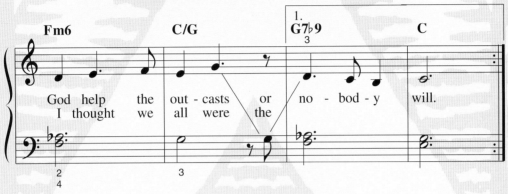

Fm6   **C/G**   **1.**   **G7♭9**   **C**

God help the out - casts or no - bod - y will.
I thought we all were the

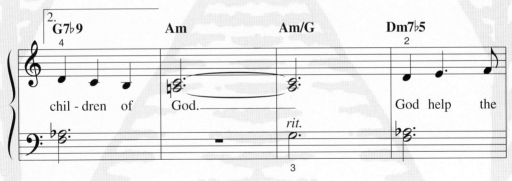

2. **G7♭9**   **Am**   **Am/G**   **Dm7♭5**

chil - dren of God. _____ God help the

rit.

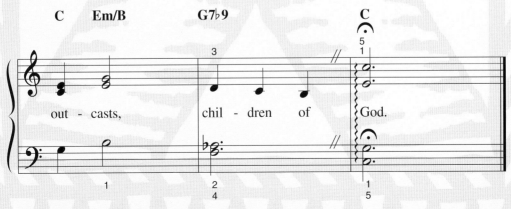

C   **Em/B**   **G7♭9**   **C**

out - casts, chil - dren of God.

GOD HELP THE OUTCASTS

Music by **Alan Menken** • Lyrics by **Stephen Schwartz**

ESMERALDA:
I don't know if You can hear me
Or if You're even there
I don't know if You would listen
To a gypsy's prayer
Yes, I know I'm just an outcast
I shouldn't speak to You
Still I see Your face and wonder
Were You once an outcast too?

God help the outcasts
Hungry from birth
Show them the mercy
They don't find on Earth
God help my people
They look to You still
God help the outcasts
Or nobody will

PARISHIONERS:
I ask for wealth
I ask for fame
I ask for glory to shine on my name
I ask for love I can possess
I ask for God and His angels to bless me

ESMERALDA:
I ask for nothing
I can get by
But I know so many
Less lucky than I
Please help my people
The poor and downtrod
I thought we all were
The children of God
God help the outcasts
Children of God

# HEAVEN'S LIGHT

HEAVEN'S LIGHT

Music by **Alan Menken**
Lyrics by **Stephen Schwartz**

Moderately, with expression

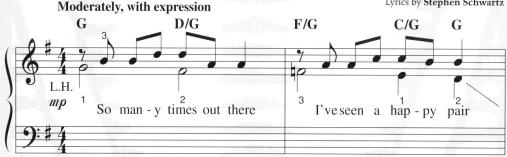

So man-y times out there   I've seen a hap-py pair

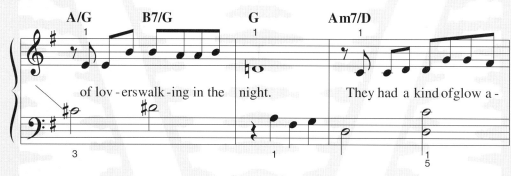

of lov-ers walk-ing in the   night.   They had a kind of glow a-

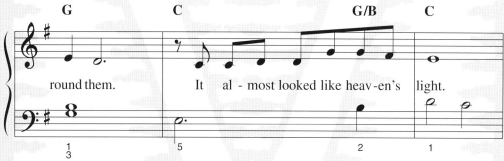

round them.   It al-most looked like heav-en's   light.

I knew I'd nev-er know   that warm and lov-ing glow,

though I might wish with all my might.

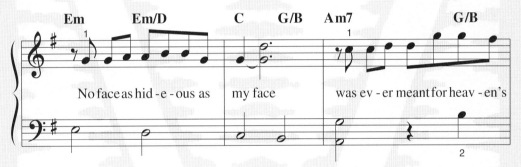

No face as hid-e-ous as my face was ev-er meant for heav-en's

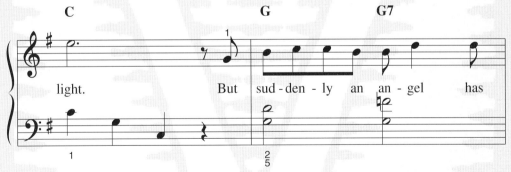

light. But sud-den-ly an an-gel has

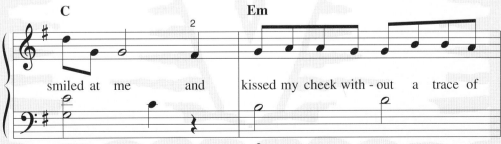

smiled at me and kissed my cheek with-out a trace of

A **D7** **G** **D/G**

fright. I dare to dream that she

F/G **C/G** **G** **A/G** **B7/G**

might e - ven care for me, and as I ring these bells to -

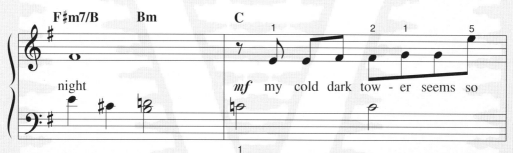

F♯m7/B **Bm** **C**

night *mf* my cold dark tow - er seems so

Bm **Em7** **Am7** **D7sus** **G**

bright. I swear it must be heav - en's light. *p*

HEAVEN'S LIGHT

Music by **Alan Menken** • Lyrics by **Stephen Schwartz**

QUASIMODO:

So many times out there
I've watched a happy pair
Of lovers walking in the night
They had a kind of glow around them
It almost looked like heaven's light

I knew I'd never know
That warm and loving glow
Though I might wish with all my might
No face as hideous as my face
Was ever meant for heaven's light

But suddenly an angel has smiled at me
And kissed my cheek without a trace of fright

I dare to dream that she
Might even care for me
And as I ring these bells tonight
My cold dark tower seems so bright
I swear it must be heaven's light

HELLFIRE

HELLFIRE

Music by **Alan Menken**
Lyrics by **Stephen Schwartz**
Latin lyrics adapted by **Stephen Schwartz**

Am   **E**   **Am**   **Dm**   **C/E**   **E**

tell me,   Ma - ri - a,   why I see her danc - ing there,

F   **B sus**   **B7**   **E**

why her smol - d'ring eyes still scorch my   soul.   I

Am   **E**   **Am**   **Dm**   **C/E**   **E**

feel her,   I see   her, the   sun caught in her ra - ven hair is

F   **B7**   **E sus**   **E**

blaz - ing in me out of all con - trol.

N.C.(A bass)

Like fi – re, hell fi – re,

this fi – re in my skin.

D

N.C.(E bass)

This burn – ing de – si – re

Bm   Gmaj7   Em

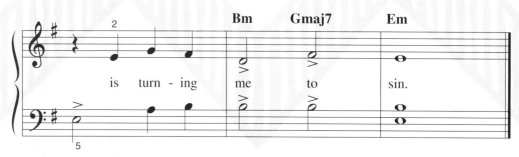

is turn – ing me to sin.

HELLFIRE

Music by **Alan Menken** • Lyrics by **Stephen Schwartz** • Latin lyrics adapted by **Stephen Schwartz**

PRIESTS:
Confiteor deo omnipotenti
  (I confess to God Almighty)
Beatae Mariae semper virgini
  (To blessed Mary eternal virgin)
Beato Michaeli archangelo
  (To the blessed archangel Michael)
Sanctis apostolis omnibus sanctis
  (To the holy apostles, to all the saints)

FROLLO:
Beata Maria
You know I am a righteous man
Of my virtue I am justly proud

PRIESTS:
Et tibi pater   (And to you, Father)

FROLLO:
Beata Maria
You know I'm so much purer than
The common, vulgar, weak, licentious
crowd

PRIESTS:
Quia peccavi nimis   (That I have
sinned)

FROLLO:
Then tell me, Maria
Why I see her dancing there
Why her smold'ring eyes still scorch
my soul

PRIESTS:
Cogitatione   (In thought)

FROLLO:
I feel her, I see her
The sun caught in her raven hair
Is blazing in me out of all control

PRIESTS:
Verbo et opere   (In word and deed)

FROLLO:
Like fire
Hellfire
This fire in my skin

This burning
Desire
Is turning me to sin

FROLLO:
It's not my fault

I'm not to blame

It is the gypsy girl
The witch who sent
this flame

It's not my faul

If in God's plan

He made the devil so much
Stronger than a man

PRIESTS:
Mea culpa
(Through my fault)
Mea culpa
(Through my fault)

Mea maxima culpa
(Through my most
grievous fault)
Mea culpa
(Through my fault)
Mea culpa
(Through my fault)

Mea maxima culpa
(Through my most
grievous fault)

Protect me, Maria
Don't let this siren cast her spell
Don't let her fire sear my flesh and bone
Destroy Esmeralda
And let her taste the fires of hell
Or else let her be mine and mine alone

Hellfire
Dark fire
Now gypsy, it's your turn
Choose me or
Your pyre
Be mine or you will burn

Kyrie Eleison
(God have mercy)
God have mercy on her   Kyrie Eleison
(God have mercy)
God have mercy on me   Kyrie Eleison
(God have mercy)

But she will be mine
Or she will burn!

 GUY LIKE YOU

A GUY LIKE YOU

Music by **Alan Menken**
Lyrics by **Stephen Schwartz**

Lyrics:
Par - is, the cit - y of lov - ers is glow - ing this eve - ning.
True, that's be - cause it's on fire — but still there's "l'a - mour."
Some - where out there in the night her heart is al - so a-

Bm7

light,

Am7 · 3 · **Bm7** · 3 ·

and I know the guy she just

Cmaj7 **C♯m7♭5** **B** **D7**

might be burn - ing for... *rit.* A guy like

Am7 **D7** **G** **Em7**

a tempo
you she's nev - er known, kid. A guy like
guys that she could dan - gle all look the

Am7 **D7** **1. G**

you a girl does not meet ev - 'ry day. You've got a
same from ev - 'ry bor - ing point of

A GUY LIKE YOU

Music by **Alan Menken** • Lyrics by **Stephen Schwartz**

HUGO:
Paris, the city of lovers
Is glowing this evening
True, that's because it's on fire
But still, there's 'l'amour'
Somewhere out there in the night
Her heart is also alight
And I know the guy she just might
Be burning for...

A guy like you
She's never known, kid
A guy like you
A girl does not meet ev'ry day
You've got a look
That's all your own, kid
Could there be two?

VICTOR AND LAWRENCE:
Like you?

ALL THREE:
No way!

HUGO:
Those other guys
That she could dangle
All look the same
From ev'ry boring point of view
You're a surprise
From ev'ry angle
Mon Dieu above
She's gotta love
A guy like you

VICTOR:
A guy like you
Gets extra credit
Because it's true
You've got a certain something more

HUGO:
You're aces, kid

LAVERNE:
You see that face
You don't forget it

VICTOR AND LAWRENCE:
Want something new?

HUGO:
That's you...

ALL THREE:
For sure!

LAVERNE:
We all have gaped
At some Adonis

VICTOR:
But then we crave a meal
More nourishing to chew...

HUGO:
And since you're shaped
Like a croissant is

ALL THREE:
No question of
She's gotta love
A guy like you!

LAVERNE:
Call me a hopeless romantic
But Quasi, I feel it

VICTOR:
She wants you so
Any moment she'll walk through the door

ALL THREE:
For

HUGO:
A guy so swell
With all you bring her
A fool could tell
It's why she fell
For you-know-who

You ring the bell

VICTOR& LAVERNE:
A guy like you
I tell you, Quasi
There never was
Another, was he
From king to serf
To the bourgeoisie
They're all a second
stringer

ALL THREE:
You're the bell ringer!
When she wants ooh-la-la
Then she wants you la-la
She will discover, guy
You're one heckuva guy
Who wouldn't love a guy
Like you?

HUGO:
You got a lot
The rest have not
So she's gotta love
A guy like you!

THE COURT OF MIRACLES

THE COURT OF MIRACLES

Music by **Alan Menken**
Lyrics by **Stephen Schwartz**

May - be you've heard of a ter - ri - ble
May - be you've heard of that myth - i - cal
We have a meth - od for spies and in -

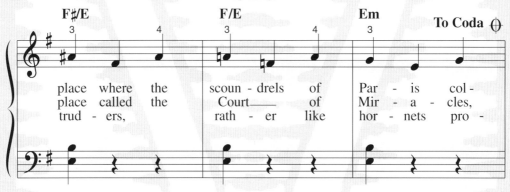

place where the scoun - drels of Par - is col -
place called the Court of Mir - a - cles,
trud - ers, rath - er like hor - nets pro -

lect in a lair.

hel - lo, you're

Bm

there! Where the lame can

B

Em

walk, and the blind can

Bm **B**

Em

see. But the dead don't

D

C

talk, so you won't be a-

F♯7 **B** D.C. al Coda

round   to   re -   veal   what   you   found.

CODA

B **C**

tect - ing   their   hive.   Here   in   the

B **Em** **F**

Court ____   of   Mir - a - cles   where   it's   a

F♯7 **B** **Em**

mir - a - cle   if   you   get   out ____   a - live.

THE COURT OF MIRACLES

Music by **Alan Menken** • Lyrics by **Stephen Schwartz**

CLOPIN AND GYPSIES:
Maybe you've heard of a terrible place
Where the scoundrels of Paris
Collect in a lair
Maybe you've heard of that mythical place
Called the Court of Miracles
Hello, you're there!
Where the lame can walk
And the blind can see
But the dead don't talk
So you won't be around
To reveal what you've found
We have a method for spies and intruders
That's rather like hornets protecting their hive
Here in the Court of Miracles
Where it's a miracle if you get out alive!

CLOPIN:
Justice is swift in the Court of Miracles
I am the lawyers and judge all in one
We like to get the trial over with quickly
Because it's the sentence that's really the fun!

Now that we've seen all the evidence...

PUPPET:
Wait! I object!

CLOPIN:
Overruled!

PUPPET:
I object!

CLOPIN:
Quiet!

PUPPET:
Dang!

CLOPIN:
We find you totally innocent...
Which is the worst crime of all...

So you're going to hang!

THE BELLS OF NOTRE DAME (REPRISE)

Music by **Alan Menken** • Lyrics by **Stephen Schwartz**

CLOPIN:
So here is a riddle to guess if you can
Sing the bells of Notre Dame
What makes a monster and what makes a man?

CHORUS:
Sing the bells, bells, bells, bells (etc.)

CLOPIN:
Whatever their pitch, you
Can feel them bewitch you
The rich and the ritual knells
Of the

CLOPIN AND CHORUS:
Bells of Notre Dame